The Great One

by Barbara A. Donovan

SCHOOL PUBLISHERS

Cover, ©File/MLB Photos via Getty Images; p.3, ©AP/Wide World Photo; p.4, ©Bettmann/CORBIS; p.5, ©Three Lions/Getty Images; p.6, ©National Baseball Hall of Fame Library/MLB Photos via Getty Images; p.7, Blank Archives/Getty Images; p.8, ©AP Photo; p.9, ©AP Photo; p.10, ©Bettmann/CORBIS; p.11, ©AP Photo; p.12, ©National Baseball Hall of Fame Library/MLB Photos via Getty Images; p.13, ©Bettmann/CORBIS; p.14, ©AP Photo/Jim McKnight.

Copyright © by Harcourt, Inc.

All rights reserved. No part of this publication may be reproduced or transmitted in any form or by any means, electronic or mechanical, including photocopy, recording, or any information storage and retrieval system, without permission in writing from the publisher.

Requests for permission to make copies of any part of the work should be addressed to School Permissions and Copyrights, Harcourt, Inc., 6277 Sea Harbor Drive, Orlando, Florida 32887-6777. Fax: 407-345-2418.

HARCOURT and the Harcourt Logo are trademarks of Harcourt, Inc., registered in the United States of America and/or other jurisdictions.

Printed in the United States of America

ISBN 10: 0-15-351082-X
ISBN 13: 978-0-15-351082-3

Ordering Options
ISBN 10: 0-15-350603-2 (Grade 6 On-Level Collection)
ISBN 13: 978-0-15-350603-1 (Grade 6 On-Level Collection)
ISBN 10: 0-15-357978-1 (package of 5)
ISBN 13: 978-0-15-357978-3 (package of 5)

If you have received these materials as examination copies free of charge, Harcourt School Publishers retains title to the materials and they may not be resold. Resale of examination copies is strictly prohibited and is illegal.

Possession of this publication in print format does not entitle users to convert this publication, or any portion of it, into electronic format.

2 3 4 5 6 7 8 9 10   179   12 11 10 09 08 07

A Dream of Baseball

Puerto Rico is a beautiful island that is noted for its beautiful beaches, warm blue waters, and friendly people. It's also known for its national sport—baseball. Due to its intense passion for baseball, Puerto Rico has also become famous for its exceptional baseball players.

"The Great One," the hero of Puerto Rico, is a man whose life is remembered not just for his sport. He is also remembered for speaking out against unfairness and for giving of himself to help others. He is none other than Roberto Clemente, one of the greatest players who ever graced a baseball diamond.

On August 18, 1934, in Puerto Rico, the Clemente family welcomed its seventh child, Roberto. Although he grew up during the Great Depression, Roberto never thought of himself or his family as poor. They always had clothes to wear and food to eat, and their home was filled with love and laughter.

Still, money was tight. Roberto's father, a foreman on a sugar plantation, earned only forty-five cents per day. This was a fairly good salary given the times, but certainly not generous. The family had what they needed to survive, but baseballs and bicycles were luxuries. Once when young Roberto wanted a used bicycle, he took a daily job carrying a heavy can of milk to a neighbor's home. He earned one cent a day. Though it took Roberto three years, he finally earned enough money to buy his bicycle.

Roberto was not afraid to work hard for what he wanted. His mother hoped her youngest son would become an engineer. However, young Roberto had other plans. He wanted to play professional baseball. From the moment he'd wake up in the morning until he fell asleep at night, Roberto had a baseball in his hand. He squeezed the ball to strengthen his grip. He'd toss the ball against the walls of his room as he lay in bed at night. He listened to baseball games on the radio. On weekends, he'd take the bus to a ballpark to watch winter league baseball games.

This love of baseball would not have paid off had Roberto not been a natural athlete. When he was fourteen, a man named Roberto Marin spotted Roberto playing ball in the street. Mr. Marin invited Roberto to play shortstop for his company's softball team. Since Roberto could propel a ball across an entire ball field, he later moved from shortstop to the outfield.

At seventeen, Roberto tried out for a professional baseball team in the Puerto Rico Winter League. A scout for the Brooklyn Dodgers was also there. Of the seventy-two ballplayers trying out that day, only one stood out. He could throw the ball 400 feet (122 m). He could run the 60-yard (55 m) dash in 6.4 seconds. He hit ten baseballs over the fence. He was Roberto Clemente. As good as he was, though, Roberto was too young. He had to wait until he was eighteen to sign with the Dodgers. Instead, he got his father's permission to play in the winter league.

A Dream Come True

Playing in the winter league from 1952–1954 gave Roberto his first professional baseball experience. Several scouts from major league baseball liked what they saw. On February 19, 1954, he signed a contract with the Brooklyn Dodgers. He would begin playing for their minor league team in Montreal, Canada. As excited as he was about starting his career with the Dodgers, Roberto soon became discouraged. He would play very well in one game. Then his manager would bench him for the next three games. Roberto was puzzled and upset.

Later, Roberto found out what was going on. The Dodgers were most likely trying to hide him from other teams who might want to sign him in the baseball draft the next year. If he didn't play often, the other teams would have no way of knowing about him. The plan didn't work. In 1954, for the third year in a row, the Pittsburgh Pirates ended up in last place. There's one good thing about coming in last. The last place team gets first pick in the baseball draft. The Pirates only wanted one player—Roberto Clemente. They selected Roberto, and he made it to the big leagues at last.

In 1955, when Roberto joined the Pirates in Fort Myers, Florida, for spring training, he was a twenty-year-old player with a lot of talent and a lot to learn. One thing he had not expected to learn about was racial prejudice. In Puerto Rico, the color of his skin did not count against him, but in the United States, it was a  different story. Segregation was new to him. He could not eat at the same restaurants as the white members of his team. He could not stay in the same hotels. Roberto was very proud of his Puerto Rican heritage. He felt astonishment and great hurt that people would treat him so unfairly purely because of the color of his skin.

Roberto was also judged harshly because of his accent. He spoke two languages—Spanish and some English. Writers who interviewed him poked fun at the way he spoke. They wrote the words he said the way they sounded. They didn't write the words he intended to say. They tried to make him sound ignorant. Because of this, he never trusted writers. He often spoke out against them and the way they and others treated him and other players of color.

In spite of the way he was treated by some, Roberto Clemente grew as a ballplayer and as a leader for the next eighteen years, from 1954–1972. His coaches tried many remedies to change the way he stood in the batter's box. They wanted to make him a better hitter. In the field, he lunged for balls headed for the wall and often ended up with cuts and bruises. He tossed balls against the corners in an unfamiliar ballpark so that he could understand how the ball would bounce off the wall. He found that if he held his glove at his waist or below, he would rarely fumble the ball. With this basket catch, the ball dropped right into his glove. He worked hard to make his game as good as could be.

In his long career with the Pirates, Roberto Clemente won many awards. He won twelve Golden Glove awards for his work as an outfielder. He represented the National League in twelve All-Star games. In thirteen seasons, he batted over .300, which means that he got a hit about three out of every ten times he came to the plate. That is considered to be an excellent batting average. He was the National League batting champ four times. Twice, in 1960 and in 1971, he helped the Pirates win the World Series. In 1966, he was named the Most Valuable Player in the National League. He was a star.

"The Great One"

Winning games and playing baseball were not the only important parts of Roberto's life. He was very much interested in helping others. He dreamed of building a sports center in Puerto Rico. He wanted a place where children could learn and play sports regardless of how rich or poor they were. He often gave his time to his community. He held baseball clinics to help young ballplayers improve their skills. He was a compassionate man who helped many people.

　In 1972, a triumphant Roberto Clemente scored his 3,000th hit in a baseball game. Only ten other major league players had done it before him. He was the first player from Puerto Rico to reach this mark. On December 23, that same year, an earthquake hit the Central American country of Nicaragua. Thousands of people were killed and injured. Not long before, Roberto had spent a month in Nicaragua and had made many friends among the people there.

Roberto could not just write a check to help the people he had called his friends. He had to do something. He started working to gather medicines, clothing, and other supplies in Puerto Rico. He worked day and night. He went door-to-door in the neighborhoods where people who were wealthy lived to get donations. He lined up planes and a ship to bring the supplies he had gathered to the people of Nicaragua.

Soon Roberto learned that people had stolen the things he had sent. He was furious. He decided to gather more supplies. This time he would take them to Nicaragua himself. December 31, 1972, was New Year's Eve, a time for celebration. That was not how Roberto planned to spend that day. Instead, he loaded a plane with supplies. Then it took off for Nicaragua with Roberto onboard. Tragically, one of the plane's engines caught on fire shortly after take-off. The plane dropped into the ocean. All five people onboard, including Roberto Clemente, died in the crash.

In 1973, Roberto Clemente became the first Latin American member of the National Baseball Hall of Fame. Because of his brilliant career in baseball, the usual five-year wait for the Hall of Fame was set aside for him.

In a 1971 speech, Roberto Clemente said something that spoke the truth about his life. He said, "Any time you have the opportunity to accomplish something for somebody who comes behind you, and you don't do it, you are wasting your time on this earth." No one who knew him could say that Roberto Clemente wasted his time on earth. To this day, his wife and children have been instrumental in keeping his legacy alive.

Think Critically

1. Why did Roberto play in the outfield for Mr. Marin's softball team?

2. Based on the information in the book, draw a time line of the key events in Roberto Clemente's life.

3. What was Roberto Clemente most likely feeling when he heard about the earthquake in Nicaragua?

4. Do you think that Roberto Clemente was right when he spoke out against the writers who poked fun at how he spoke? Explain your answer.

5. How do you think the author feels about Roberto Clemente? What clues in the book helped you decide?

 Social Studies

Write a Television Bulletin Write a bulletin for a television announcer to read about Roberto Clemente being inducted into the National Baseball Hall of Fame. Look on the Internet or in other library resources for more information about this event.

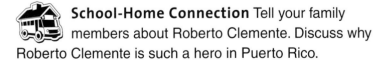 **School-Home Connection** Tell your family members about Roberto Clemente. Discuss why Roberto Clemente is such a hero in Puerto Rico.

Word Count: 1,606